Granny's Namesake

Donna Honc

Archway Publishing books may be ordered through booksellers or by contacting:

Archway Publishing
1663 Liberty Drive
Bloomington, IN 47403
www.archwaypublishing.com
1 (888) 242-5904

Because of the dynamic nature of the Internet, any web addresses or links contained in this book may have changed since publication and may no longer be valid. The views expressed in this work are solely those of the author and do not necessarily reflect the views of the publisher, and the publisher hereby disclaims any responsibility for them.

Any people depicted in stock imagery provided by Getty Images are models, and such images are being used for illustrative purposes only.
Certain stock imagery © Getty Images.

3 images from REDDOOR Studios.

ISBN: 978-1-4808-7502-9 (sc)
ISBN: 978-1-4808-7503-6 (hc)
ISBN: 978-1-4808-7504-3 (e)

Print information available on the last page.

Archway Publishing rev. date: 3/8/2019

To my daughter, Lilli-Anne, who has brought joy unspeakable to my heart. And to a very special lady whose life and testimony has been an inspiration to me, and whose legacy of faith and love will continue to inspire generations to come—the dearest mother-in-law, Lillian Honc.

Acknowledgments

This book would not be in your hands today without the encouragement and technical support of my daughter Alexandra. You always encourage me to follow my dreams.

Thank you to my daughter Crystal Robertson and to Marie Kamp of REDDOOR Studios in Fort Myers, Florida, for capturing the moments of our lives.

Prologue

At the age of three, Lilli-Anne's curiosity sent her on a quest for answers to her questions. Like "Why was I named after Granny? Is it because we are so much alike—or because we look alike?" She arrived at many possible conclusions, many of which had some truth to them. After exhausting all the reasons her three-year-old mind could come up with about why she was named after Granny, she decided to ask her mom. Her mom's answer, at that time, was not really understood by little Lilli, but she knew one day she would understand completely.

On the day I was born, my mama and daddy named me Lilli-Anne, after my granny Lillian. That makes me her namesake.

Being the baby in a family of six, with two brothers and three older sisters, I often wondered why I was chosen to be Granny's namesake. But at the age of three, the reasons soon became clear to me.

First of all, Granny and I look just alike. Daddy says our eyes are as blue and clear as Charlotte Harbor, and our golden locks remind him of a summer sun setting over Boca Grande Pass. Our skin is as fair as the lilies we're named for, and our dimples could swallow a ship at sea when we laugh.

aughing is something that Granny and I do a lot of, always with our heads tilted back. We always throw our whole selves into everything we do. Granny says every day is a reason for celebrating, and what's a celebration without food, music, and dancing? Granny's always humming a tune or singing while she works. We like songs about Jesus, but I like them loud. Mama says my sense of rhythm comes from Granny. At parties, we're the last ones on the dance floor, cutting a rug—whatever that means.

My granny sees life as one big adventure. She daydreams a lot about places she's never seen and trails she's yet to blaze.

Mama says Granny and Papa's theme song should be "Ain't No Mountain High Enough" because they've climbed some steep ones. I didn't know they liked mountain climbing; we live in Florida. It must be something they do on those motor home trips they take. Perhaps I should go along the next time. I like adventure too, and they may need my help before long. But Daddy says not to worry; God is their help in times of trouble. What does that have to do with mountain climbing?

There is a place that Granny and I love to share with Papa. Nestled among sand pines, scrub oaks, and palmettos is a little dollhouse Papa calls a hunting cabin. This is where Granny and I play house while Papa hunts. We cook good-smelling dinners and have a cozy fire burning and oil lamps lit when Papa comes home. Papa goes without us sometimes, but he likes it best when we're there.

Sometimes Papa takes us for rides on his big hunting buggy, and we always end up in the middle of a flag pond, where cattails and wild lilies grow. Where else would he go with two wild lilies on board? Papa says we're like two peas in a pod. Whatever that means.

"Look your best at all times"; that's my granny's motto. My love for makeup surely comes from her. We both adore blue eye shadow. Fire-engine-red lipstick is our favorite color, and we wear it at all times. Granny puts it on even if it's just me coming to visit and always before Papa comes home. I always go home with "Granny kisses" all over my face.

I don't know how one person can have such opposite effects on people. Mama says she has aged ten years since I was born, and Granny says I'm her secret weapon against aging, that I keep her young. Whatever that means.

Granny and I like to do things fast. My granny can work circles around anyone I know. I can clean my play kitchen and Mama's real kitchen in half the time it takes my sisters.

*B*oredom comes easily for us, so we are always thinking of new things to do and games to play. Then we play them fast and move on to the next experience. Daddy says we even fall asleep fast. Some people would say we are hyper, but Granny says we are just fast oxidizers. Whatever that means.

Sometimes on my visits to Granny's we just swing on the porch and talk. Of course, these talks always include cherry Popsicles, and most of the time I have two, but Granny never told. Mama said Granny is my "secret keeper," but where does she keep them?

*B*esides my mama and daddy, no one knows me better than Granny. And she says there is not one thing she would change about me. She says I am worth my weight in gold. Whatever that means.

*J*ust when I thought I knew why I was chosen as Granny's namesake, I asked Mama one day, "Why did you wait to name me after Granny?"

Her answer was simple. "Well, honey, I guess it took me this long to realize what a special lady she is, and how much she means to me."

About the Author

Donna and Dan, her husband of forty-two years, live in a close-knit island community on Florida's Gulf Coast. Four generations of their family are native to this quaint fishing paradise, including their six children and several of their eleven grandchildren. *Granny's Namesake* was written almost twenty years ago as a gift to the  author's three-year-old daughter and her mother-in-law. The book has been read over the years to her children and grandchildren. The pursuit to publish *Granny's Namesake* became the author's passion after the passing of her mother-in-law, Lillian Frances Honc, on December 12, 2017. Lillian's love for her family and her faith in God are legacies that each generation will carry with them.

CPSIA information can be obtained
at www.ICGtesting.com
Printed in the USA
BVHW060526190319
542960BV00016B/1301/P